BEAUTIFUL TREES

COLORING BOOK

Tim Foley

DOVER PUBLICATIONS, INC.
MINEOLA, NEW YORK

When we think of trees, their beauty and grandeur often come to mind first. But the longer we reflect on the subject, the more value we see. Trees produce oxygen, help prevent erosion, provide homes for animals, and buffer the wind—some even produce fruits for us to enjoy! This new coloring book includes illustrations of all kinds of trees, from the majestic cedar to the elegant palm to the delicate bonsai, and more. The name of each tree is provided in a caption, giving you the opportunity to learn while you color! Try different media and techniques as you progress through the book. Each of the thirty-one plates has been perforated for removal to make displaying your work easy.

Bibliographical Note
Beautiful Trees Coloring Book is a new work,
first published by Dover Publications, Inc., in 2017.

International Standard Book Number
ISBN-13: 978-0-486-81540-4
ISBN-10: 0-486-81540-4

Manufactured in the United States by LSC Communications
81540401   2016
www.doverpublications.com